"She creates grace in her own image,
brings Heaven to earth
in one movement of her hand."

~ Edmond Rostad
(from Cyrano de Bergerac)

Also by James Roethlein

Musing on the Cricket Game of Life Part 1 and 1/2

An Extravagant Way of Saying Nothing

Letters to Roxanne

James Roethlein

Silver Bow Publishing

720 Sixth Street, Unit #5
New Westminster, BC
V3L 3C5
CANADA

Title: Letters to Roxanne
Author: James Roethlein
Publisher: Silver Bow Publishing
Cover Layout and Design: Candice James
Editing: Candice James

All rights reserved including the right to reproduce or translate this book or any portions thereof, in any form without the permission of the publisher. Except for the use of short passages for review purposes, no part of this book may be reproduced, in part or in whole, or transmitted in any form or by any means, either by means electronically or mechanically, including photocopying, recording, or any information or storage retrieval system without prior permission in writing from the publisher or a licence from the Canadian Copyright Collective Agency (Access Copyright).

www.silverbowpublishing.com
info@silverbowpublishing.com
ISBN: 978-1-77403-207-7 paperback
ISBN: 978-1-77403-208-4 electronic book
© 2022 Silver Bow Publishing

Library and Archives Canada Cataloguing in Publication
waiting for CIP

Letters to Roxanne

To my own personal Roxanne

Letters to Roxanne

Contents

I Told the Sun About You ... 9
Every Poem I've Written for You ... 10
Hope is Dancing ... 11
Twilight and the Dawn ... 12
I Look at You ... 13
I've Given My Heart ... 14
She Is The Days ... 15
She Comes As Sunshine ... 16
Sing Your Life's Story ... 17
Extraordinary Moments of the Mundane ... 18
Lovely Lady ... 19
I Want To ... 20
12 Labors ... 21
She Is Something More ... 22
The Court Jester ... 23
Sweet 16 Ways ... 24
Aries in Love ... 25
She is the Goddess ... 26
Meadow Charmed Woman ... 27
Emerald Eyed Lady ... 28
Her Eyes Are Rivers ... 29
Borrow My Breath ... 30
You Are ... 31
How Does One...? ... 32
Just to Say Hello ... 33
Let Me Be ... 34
Rest Here My Darling ... 35
Miles Turn Into Inches ... 36
Emerald-Eyes of May ... 37
I See Your Eyes ... 38
Hearts Drawing Closer ... 39
Be the Morning to Me ... 40
Her Name Means Hope ... 41
To ... 42
He Touches Her Gently ... 43

My Lady Love ... 44
Rainbow Beautiful ... 45
Goddess of Midnight Visions ... 46
Hope Face Shining ... 47
Forty Six Words ... 48
Pen to Paper ... 49
He Sees Stars ... 50
A Word from You ... 51
Meadow Fields ... 52
Extraordinary Displays of the Mundane Pt 2 ... 53
As An Angel on Earth ... 54
Precious To My Eyes ... 55
She is as a Gift from God ...56
I Surrender ... 57
She is Hope ... 58
I Hear Hope in Your Name ... 59
Heart Felt ... 60
Sometimes Loving You ... 61
She Sings Sweet ... 62
Perhaps He is to Her ... 63
Silence Cuts Me ... 64
The Morning I Saw in You ... 65
How Long I Have Longed ... 66
Winter To Her Summer ... 67
I Argued With The Moon ... 68

I Told the Sun About You

I told the Sun about you,
how your inner beauty
radiates light and warmth
to the world around you.
And the Sun simply said,
treasure her.

Every Poem I've Written for You

Love and affection,
words whispered
upon a printed page
and written as sound
for mortal ears to hear.
Three words felt,
coursing thru the veins
of every poem I've written
for you
for you.

Hope is Dancing

Lying alone each night, empty arms aching,
all the while
hope is dancing
hope is dancing
hope is dancing
in my dreams
when I'm awake I would seek to see
the sunshine in your face
the heavens in your eyes
and to hear the melodic honey of your lips
that would turn my lemonade soul sweet.

And I would hope
And I would hope
And I would hope
you'd dance duet with me
all the years we have left.

Twilight and the Dawn

She is
twilight
She is
the dawn
nights
of wonder,
days
of dreams.
As spring
is to winter,
she is rain
to the thirsty,
and his heart
will drink in her love.

I Look at You

I look at you
and I see you, now,
weather worn,
deep blue ember eyes
beautiful thru and thru,
with loving tender hands
and a Phoenix heart
ever rising from the fires
life is throwing your way.
And I love you
    I love you
    I love you.

I've Given My Heart

I've given my heart to hope,
fully flesh, far beyond beauty
in surface and soul,
for you have softened me
from granite to soapstone,
and warmed me to the core.
So let me hold you,
(my lady, and my love)
with arms to help you
weather your every storm.

She Is The Days

She is the days, the hours,
the months and the seasons,
emerald eyes, moonbeam hair,
time worn, wise, and beautiful,
Roxanne is in Cyrano's dreams
dancing, dancing, dancing
to a tune only they could know.

She Comes As Sunshine

She comes as sunshine,
pushing against shadows
of love's long winter,
midnight upon his brow.
And he asks if he could be
the beacon light leading
to the bridge above the gulf
of her troubled waters.

Sing Your Life's Story

Sing your life's story
and duet
with my spoken word,
two voices beautiful
slow dancing on the stage,
hands held, hearts entwined,
for the world to look on
and envy what it sees.

Extraordinary Moments of the Mundane

Live
Laugh
Love
smile and cry,
stepping
from dreams,
Ruth is at
the threshing floor
holding hands together,
to live out
the extraordinary moments
of the mundane.

Lovely Lady

Lovely lady
with a velvet heart
and velvet hands,
her eyes
soft as soapstone,
precious as diamonds.
And a poet
longs to kiss her,
for what he feels
is love like an ocean,
far too deep
to be held in a poem.

I Want To

I want to write you into a poem,
wrap you in meter and rhyme,
that I may present you
both body and soul
in spoken word fashion,
for your face to me is metaphor
and your voice to me is rhythm
with eyes still windows to the soul

12 Labors

Twelve labors,
just to see you smile,
I would fight the world
for a night in your arms.
For you are Helen, you are Ruth,
and I would face death
from a thousand spears,
for a lifetime of your affections.

She Is Something More

She is something more
than the stars will ever be,
as close as they are distant
and warmer than the sun.
Life is shining in her eyes,
so majestic on her face
strength found in her frame
as love flows in her voice.
A treasure to be cherished
by men, not fools and boys.

The Court Jester

The court jester in shadows
standing beyond the glow
of throne-room torches,
so in love
so in love
so in love with his Queen,
for she is to him
hope in human flesh,
beautiful to her soul,
and he asks
and he asks
and he asks to be her Prince.

Sweet 16 Ways

Sweet 16 ways
of how
of how
I adore you,
this is number 17,
and I shall never stop
telling
telling
how I feel about you.

Aries in Love

Aries in love
with a Gemini woman,
moonbeam emerald eyes
and star shine in her face.
He gives her his heart
a treasure for her to hold,
as he holds her heart in his.

She is the Goddess

She is the goddess
of morning kisses,
of morning smiles,
and I am one longing
(for a thousandfold days)
to be lost in her sunrise eyes.

Meadow Charmed Woman

In her heart
she is mountain meadows
and tulip fields,
daisies, daffodils, red roses,
and pink carnations.
To step inside her world
that I may know her,
prickly pear, black dahlia,
rose of Sharon,
and lily of the valley.

She is meant to be loved
She deserves to be loved.

Emerald-Eyed Lady

Emerald-eyed lady,
she is as moonlight
with the warmth of the sun,
her hope heart, loved
by a man of sea spray eyes,
soul shadows lessened
as hearts and hands touch,
drawn closer to each other
all the years before them
that God has ordained.

Her Eyes Are Rivers

Her eyes are rivers running
to the deep ocean of her soul,
her arms and legs
are mountains and valleys,
nature's splendor, manifest
in her female form.

Borrow My Breath

Borrow my breath
let me borrow yours,
two bodies in shared orbit
tracing each other's topography.
Touch me tenderly
and I will touch you,
taste my lips in lip lock
and I will do the same.
Let linger the moments
seeing the heavens in our eyes,
and lady, love me back
the way I love you.

You Are

You are hope dancing in my dreams,
more to me than a mere muse,
like a river flowing to meet the ocean
my heart yearns for you.
Be hope to me in my waking days
a salve to heal, and let me be the same.

How Does One...?

How does one tickle
and make you laugh?
A night of humor
and casual sensuality,
where we cuddle,
where we kiss,
where we enjoy
each other's company.

Just to Say Hello

A gentle kiss just to say hello
tender, full and passionate
she in turn holds him tight
so he'll never let her go.

Let Me Be

Let me be your pillow
let me be your bed
let me be the place
you rest your pretty head,
let my warmth mingle
with your female fire
and let me be the lover
of whom you'll never tire.

Rest Here My Darling

Rest here my darling,
rest here in my arms
while the sun is sleeping,
the moon standing guard,
use me as a pillow
to lay your precious head on,
that I may feel your heartbeat
upon my naked chest,
dream your dreams of rainbows
and doves descending from above,
til the morning wakes you
knowing you are loved.

Miles Turn Into Inches

Miles turn into inches
and minutes from days
time and distance diminished
by hearts and souls entwined,
and I would wish in this moment
for an eternity of endless days,
that I may hold you in my arms
and lose myself in your eyes.

Emerald-Eyes of May

Her emerald eyes of May,
touching mine of aquamarine
as two stones in a setting,
the sea and renewal,
together, in the waves.

I See Your Eyes

I see your eyes
and I love your eyes,
and I long
from dusk til dawn
of being with the woman
they belong to.

Hearts Drawing Closer

Hearts drawing closer
than where nostalgia lies,
and far away turns to nearby,
faces gazing into each other's eyes.

Be the Morning to Me

Be the morning to me,
the afternoon, the evening,
and walk, hand in hand
from spring to summer,
autumn then winter
(guided by time woven strands)
And let me gaze
upon your beauty found deep,
reflections of celestial splendor
and eternity residing in your eyes

Her Name Means Hope

Her name means hope,
she walks in beauty
(in my dreams)
skin deep and deeper
with window soul eyes
that I drink,
that I drink
and lose myself in.

To

To hold you
To touch you
To love you
To gaze into your eyes
To see how deep your beauty goes.

He Touches Her Gently

He touches her gently,
lifting her chin
that they may lock eyes
and stare into each other's eternity.

My Lady Love

Lie down beside me
my Lady Love,
under star-filled skies,
with the midnight hour
being our only blanket.
And rest your head
beneath my chin,
sighing contented sighs
nestled in my arms,
safe under the stars.

Rainbow Beautiful

Rainbow beautiful,
prism refracted light,
when she comes,
when she comes,
his arms outstretched,
open, longing, waiting
for the moment to hold
and be held by her.

Goddess of Midnight Visions

You are the goddess
of my midnight visions,
moonbeam eyes
and moonlight hair
pierce the blackness,
casting moon-shadows
upon the sea spray air
as you take my hand,
to dance and lie with me
in the ocean surf.
This is the moment I long for,
this is place I'd wish to be,
where dreams and reality
collide, and become one.

Hope Face Shining

Hope face shining
in midnight skies,
silver eyes,
moonlight hair,
ravens cry
carrying the call, of
he loves you
he loves you.

Forty-Six Words

Forty-six words to woo you,
a poem to pull you close
that I may kiss you tenderly,
that I may hold your hand.
This poet is here before you,
hoping, longing, for fantasy
to fly far from the page,
and become a part of real life.

Pen to Paper

The poet puts pen to paper
of the tens of thousands of ways
the Sahara could never contain
the vastness of his love for her.

He Sees Stars

He sees stars in her eyes
when they smile
and weeps beside her
when they frown,
for she is his missing rib,
and he is the rib cage
preventing her heart
from breaking.

A Word from You

A word from you
and I'm breaking the dishes
of all my days
before hope came calling
to a life lived beyond the rainbow
in the wake
of the storms we've both endured.

Meadow Fields

Meadow fields,
sunlight and wildflowers
for open armed lovers
to run across, she
and whoever he may be
in movie moment embraces
ending in happily ever afters
and ordinary days.

Extraordinary Displays of the Mundane Pt 2

Kisses in moonlight
the color of her hair,
bedtime caresses
til daybreak dawns
and they embrace
in morning moments
of the extraordinary
displays of the mundane.

As An Angel on Earth

She is to me
as an angel on Earth,
wings unseen,
but still she soars,
and with tones,
both major and minor
of melody and harmony,
she sings
        sings
                sings.

Precious To My Eyes

Precious to my eyes,
your soul as diamonds,
my lady, my love,
you are where my heart is,
you are whom I call my home,
and if you should leave,
the shadows will beckon,
beckon once more
come back here to live
come back here to hide.

She is as a Gift from God

She is as a gift from God
with eyes of earth,
moonbeams upon her face
and midnight in her hair.
The star of the sea
is smiling celestial smiles,
at music of the bishop's home,
sound flowing to the ocean.

I Surrender

I surrender
to feelings felt
for you
for you,
moments together
crying rainbows,
weeping thunderstorms,
joy and sorrow
shared heart to heart
in a lifetime with you.

She is Hope

She is hope,
precious, priceless
as Persian pottery,
guilded, painted,
beautiful without
beautiful within.

I Hear Hope in Your Name

I hear hope in your name
and see it in your eyes,
are you springtime come
to end love's winter in me?
Draw me in to hand's width away
that I may supplant your heart's pain,
and together be each other's balm
as the summer of our years draws nigh.

Heart Felt

Heart felt
I unfold
I unfold
for you
for you
for you.
And in time's turning,
will you do the same
for me?

Sometimes Loving You

Sometimes loving you
means rainy days
and thunderstorms,
but there are also days
when you're sunshine
when you're moonbeams,
and sometimes loving me
means the earthquakes
and the tidal waves
bordering my Pacific Ocean.

She Sings Sweet

She sings sweet,
love songs, whispered
to the winds of the world,
I listen and wait
and wait
and wait,
for her to sing to me.

Perhaps He is to Her

Perhaps he is to her,
more La Mancha than Lancelot,
dented armor and a rusted sword,
but not a fool fighting windmills
when she is to be protected
at the risk of his life and limb.
And while he is all too often
more jester than shining knight,
he would love her
               love her
                          love her

Silence Cuts Me

Silence cuts me to the quick,
I bleed
I bleed,
my heart is in your hands,
I do not ask
I do not ask,
that you give it back,
it is yours
it is yours.

The Morning I Saw in You

The morning I saw in you,
another midnight in winter,
spring and summer still so far away
as a blizzard comes to bury me.
A single solitary shadow
is standing in the moonlight,
for I am alone, longing for a touch,
from someone who was never there.

How Long I Have Longed

How long I have longed
for your name tied to my tongue
to taste the kisses
your lips leave lingering on mine

Will you speak to me,
angry words and loving words
to make my ears bleed
then soothe them?

You were hope to me, to be
beheld, loved beyond measure,
but having walked away from you,
is that where I must remain?

Winter To Her Summer

He is winter
to her summer soul,
his Jotunheim heart
bringing nothing,
but ice and blizzards
to the green trees
and full flowered fields
of her world.

I Argued With The Moon

I argued with the Moon
for seven days, seven nights,
til it conceded and agreed,
that you, my lady, my love,
shine brighter than when it's full.

www.ingramcontent.com/pod-product-compliance
Lightning Source LLC
Chambersburg PA
CBHW062157100526
44589CB00014B/1857